PRIMARY SOURCES OF THE THIRTEEN COLONIES AND THE LOST COLONY ™

A Primary Source History of the Colony of
GEORGIA

LIZ SONNEBORN

rosen central
Primary Source™

The Rosen Publishing Group, Inc., New York

Published in 2006 by The Rosen Publishing Group, Inc.
29 East 21st Street, New York, NY 10010

Library of Congress Cataloging-in-Publication Data

Sonneborn, Liz.
A primary source history of the Colony of Georgia/Liz Sonneborn.—1st ed.
    p. cm.—(Primary sources of the thirteen colonies and the Lost Colony)
Includes bibliographical references and index.
ISBN 1-4042-0426-1 (lib. bdg.)
ISBN 1-4042-0674-4 (pbk.)
1. Georgia—History—Colonial period, ca. 1600-1775—Juvenile literature. 2. Georgia—History—1775-1865—Juvenile literature. 3. Georgia—History—Colonial period, ca. 1600-1775—Sources—Juvenile literature. 4. Georgia—History—1775-1865—Sources—Juvenile literature. I. Title. II. Series.
F289.S68 2006
975.8'02—dc22

2004029317

Manufactured in the United States of America

On the cover: Peter Gordon, one of the first settlers of the colony of Georgia, engraved *A View of Savanah* [sic] as it stood on March 29, 1734. Gordon's print shows James Oglethorpe's module design of the city, which was based on a square-shaped unit called a ward. At the middle of each ward was a large, open space called a square, and the four corners of each ward contained a "tything." Each tything included ten house lots, which held the homes of the settlers. On the east and west sides of the square were four bigger lots, called the trustees' lots, which were the lots for public buildings such as churches, banks, or governmental buildings.

CONTENTS

INTRODUCTION

Founding Savannah

On November 17, 1732, about 115 people set sail from England on a ship called the *Ann*. After two months at sea, they had reached the South Carolina coast. At Port Royal, they were finally able to disembark the *Ann* and set foot again on solid ground.

There, the English travelers gathered for Sunday services. The minister told them to give thanks to God. But his listeners hardly needed this instruction. They were already grateful just to be alive. After the minister delivered his sermon, they all celebrated their good fortune of surviving their journey. Together, they sat down for a great feast, all having their fill of pork, turkey, and beef washed down with gulps of punch and beer.

The travelers' journey, however, was not over. On January 30, 1733, they set out in six boats, sailing down the Savannah River. Two days later, they reached the foot of Yamacraw Bluff. Their leader, James Oglethorpe, had carefully chosen this spot. Atop the bluff, they would build the first settlement in Georgia, the thirteenth English colony established in North America.

The location seemed perfect. Situated along the Savannah, it was a short boat trip away from the English settlements to the north in South Carolina. It was also close to the lands of the Yamacraws, a small group of Native Americans who belonged to the powerful Creek confederacy of tribes. Oglethorpe had already met with Tomochichi, the leader of the Yamacraws. Tomochichi welcomed the Georgians and hoped they could become allies and trading partners.

This detail from a 1735 map of the Savannah area depicts the planned community, in which colonists were given a lot of 5 acres (2 hectares) for a garden near the edge of town and 45 acres (18 ha) in the countryside for a farm. Although there were some restrictions on large land holdings, generally everyone received the same amount of land.

The area surrounding the bluff was rich in resources. All around were forests of pine trees, providing the wood the colonists would need to construct houses and other buildings. Nearby, there was plenty of freshwater as well. And the bluff was on high ground. Because of its elevation, a settlement there would be protected both from flooding and from enemy attack.

On their first night at Yamacraw Bluff, the Georgians crowded into four large tents. Oglethorpe, however, chose to stay outside, keeping watch by the light of a fire. As he looked over the river, he must have marveled that his dream of building a colony was so close to coming true. But Georgia was not only Oglethorpe's dream. For decades, creating the colony was an idea that had excited the imaginations of the English, both in the mother country and in its faraway colonies.

CHAPTER 1

A Home for the Poor

Oglethorpe's followers were far from the first settlers in the area they called Georgia. For centuries, Georgia had been the home of the Creeks. Other large Native American groups lived nearby. The Cherokees' homeland was located to the north, while the Choctaws' and Chickasaws' lay to the west.

The first Europeans in Georgia were Spanish. They arrived there about 150 years before the English. The Spanish established several forts and missions in Georgia, but their stronghold in the area was St. Augustine in present-day Florida. This town, founded in 1565, was the first permanent European settlement in North America.

In the mid-sixteenth century, the French also had their eye on Georgia and Florida. They sent several expeditions into the region. At times, the French and the Spanish battled one another, with each side hoping to drive the other out forever.

A New Colony

The English soon entered the fray. In 1653, settlers arrived in Carolina, creating a new English colony. (In 1729, the colony was split in two, and the parts were renamed North Carolina and South Carolina.) According to its charter, Carolina included lands in present-day Georgia that the Spanish claimed. From time to time, the Spanish sent soldiers into Carolina to protect their territory. Still, in a 1670 treaty of peace signed in Madrid, England and Spain agreed that whoever settled the area first would be considered its rightful owner.

As a humanitarian, James Edward Oglethorpe (1696–1785), pictured here in a portrait that was based on a 1744 painting, lived up to the Georgia trustees' motto *Non sibi sed aliis*, "Not for self, but for others." While living in London, he tirelessly toiled to reform prisons after the death of a friend who was jailed for indebtedness and who contracted smallpox there. In the colony of Georgia, Oglethorpe actively worked for the common good of the colonists and permitted religious minorities to settle there. He opposed slavery and respected the Native Americans who lived in the colony, and even tried to protect them from dishonest white traders.

The Carolinians built a thriving settlement at Charles Town. But, with the area to the south unsettled, they constantly worried about Spanish attacks. The settlers at Charles Town were also nervous about the French to the west. Charles Town was an important trading center, where the English and Native Americans met to exchange goods. The Carolinians feared the French wanted to take over this lucrative Native American trade.

In the 1720s, Carolina leaders campaigned in England for the establishment of a new colony south of Charles Town. They argued that such a colony would be a buffer, guarding Carolina from its French and Native American enemies. At the same time, several prominent Englishmen also hoped to create a colony, but for different reasons. These philanthropists wanted to help the poor of

In the Charter of Georgia (1732), King George II of Great Britain established the colony and created its governing board. The king granted James Oglethorpe and twenty associates, who were called the trustees, interest to all the land "between the Savannah and Altamaha Rivers from the Atlantic coast to the headwaters of these streams and thence to the South Seas" for twenty-one years. The trustees were not allowed to own land, hold office, or profit from the colony in any way. For a partial transcription of the charter, see page 53.

London and to solve a social problem that they feared by sending them to an English colony where they could get a fresh start in life.

The Trustees

Among these men was James Oglethorpe. Hailing from a wealthy family, Oglethorpe was elected to the British parliament in 1722. He became the chairman of a committee assigned with investigating conditions in English jails. At the time, people were often sent to jail if they failed to pay their debts. Oglethorpe was shocked by the horrible state of debtors' prisons. Because of his reports on these prisons, thousands of debtors were released. Oglethorpe's concern

MAKING SILK

Georgia's trustees demanded that colonists plant 100 mulberry trees for every 10 acres (4 ha) of land they cleared for farming. The trustees were not interested in replenishing Georgia's forests. Instead, they wanted to create a silk industry in the colony. Mulberry leaves are the primary food of silkworms. These moth larvae secrete a liquid that is used to make the thread of silk fabric. Georgia eventually produced some silk, but the industry was never as profitable as the trustees had hoped. Still, the silkworm was featured prominently on the colony's official seal.

for these debtors led him to get involved with the movement for establishing an American colony for the English poor.

In the summer of 1732, English king George II granted a charter for a new colony named after himself. Georgia was to include all lands between the Savannah and the Altamaha rivers. The king placed the responsibility for overseeing the colony in the hands of twenty-one men, including James Oglethorpe. These trustees would have nearly complete control over Georgia for just twenty-one years. After that, it would become a royal colony operated directly by the English monarch.

The charter also stipulated that trustees work for the colony for free. They were not allowed to hold office or own land in Georgia. The trustees' only reward was the satisfaction of helping the less fortunate.

Finding Colonists

Immediately, the trustees began looking for suitable people to send to Georgia. They put notices in London newspapers, asking

William Verelst painted *James Oglethorpe Presenting the Yamacraw Indians to the Georgia Trustees* around 1734–1735. After Oglethorpe returned to England, he introduced a delegation of Native Americans, including Chief Tomochichi (pictured at the right with his right arm extended), to the trustees on July 3, 1734. King George II had granted Georgia's twenty-one trustees, who were noblemen and gentlemen, a period of twenty-one years to govern it.

the "unfortunate poor" to apply. The trustees were flooded with applications. To many applicants, the deal the trustees offered must have seemed too good to be true. The trustees promised to pay for the colonists' passage. Once they got to Georgia, the colonists received free land, plus all the supplies, tools, and food they would need for one year.

With so many to choose from, the trustees selected only the most able-bodied and enthusiastic candidates. Despite Oglethorpe's interest in helping debtors, very few were picked. Most colonists were tradesmen and laborers who had fallen on hard times. None of those chosen were soldiers or sailors, even though the colonists would be expected to defend Georgia against attack. In those days, professional soldiers were often disreputable men—not the sort of people the trustees wanted for their colony.

The trustees also decided not to choose experienced farmers. They were considered too important to England's economy to send away. But this decision seemed to undermine one of the trustees' primary goals for the colony. Part of the reason the king granted the charter was the trustees' plan for making it profitable. They wanted the colonists to grow or produce items England traditionally had imported from other countries. These included silk, wine, spices, and olives. The trustees believed that by producing these goods, the colonists would become economically self-sufficient. Eventually, they would no longer have to depend on the trustees' financial support.

In late 1732, the trustees had just begun raising funds for the colony. Even so, Oglethorpe pushed them to begin their venture as soon as possible. By the fall, about 120 colonists were ready to head off for Georgia. The only trustee among them was Oglethorpe. He felt the colonists needed a strong leader, and he intended to take on the role himself.

CHAPTER 2

I n late 1732, Oglethorpe and his Georgia colonists were on board the *Ann*. The ship bobbed along the ocean for weeks with no land in sight. For the most part, the sea voyage was comfortable. The weather was good, few passengers became ill, and their stores of beef, pork, and vegetables kept the colonists well fed.

But the Georgians were probably most fortunate in having Oglethorpe as their informal leader. He helped nurse the sick and encouraged anyone who began to express doubts about his or her adventure. When a baby boy named Georgius was born, the parents asked Oglethorpe to be his godfather. Everyone on board celebrated Georgius's birth with a special supper, during which they toasted the trustees' health and the success of the colony.

Settling In

Building Savannah

After two months on the water, the *Ann* reached Charles Town. Oglethorpe went ashore and met with South Carolina's governor, Robert Johnson. He welcomed Oglethorpe and offered to give the Georgians cattle, rice, boats, and other things they would need while building their colony.

After scouting the area, Oglethorpe chose the site for Georgia's first settlement, which the Georgians called Savannah. The colonists set to work. They cleared the town site of pine trees, made the trunks into timber for houses, and built a palisade, or wooden fence, around the settlement for protection in

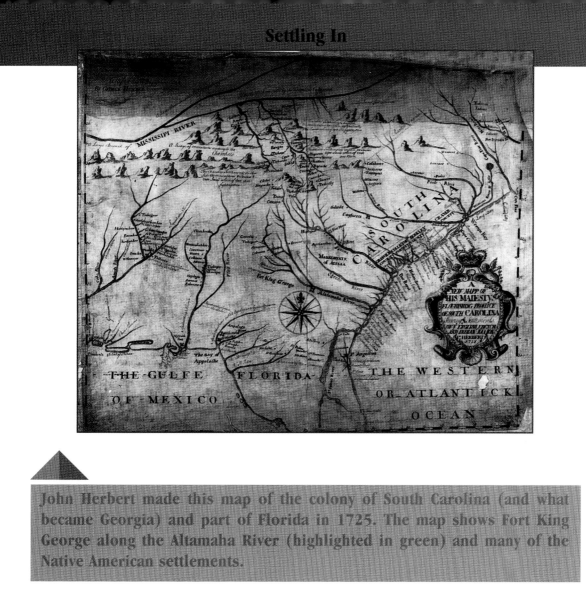

John Herbert made this map of the colony of South Carolina (and what became Georgia) and part of Florida in 1725. The map shows Fort King George along the Altamaha River (highlighted in green) and many of the Native American settlements.

case the colonists were attacked by Native Americans. Just a week after their arrival, Oglethorpe wrote a letter to England, claiming, "I have marked out the Town and Common; half of the former is already cleared, and the first House was begun Yesterday in the Afternoon."

A Charles Town merchant was one of Savannah's first visitors. He marveled that Oglethorpe was well loved by his followers despite his stern discipline. The merchant later wrote, "It is surprising to see how chearfully the Men go to work, considering they have not been bred to it. There are no Idlers there; even the Boys and Girls do their Parts."

JOHN WESLEY

One of the most famous people among Georgia's early setters was John Wesley. With his brother Charles, Wesley arrived in Georgia in 1735 and Frederica in 1736. An Anglican minister, he hoped to convert nearby Native Americans to Christianity, but instead, at Oglethorpe's request, he went to work at Savannah's church. Wesley was well liked by his congregation. He became particularly friendly with a young woman named Sophie Hopkey. After she married another man, he refused to give her and her husband Holy Communion, possibly because he was jealous. The situation caused a scandal, and Wesley returned to England in October 1737. Back home, Wesley reexamined his faith, which led him to found the Methodist Church.

New Settlers

The Georgians hustled to clear fields and plant them with wheat, vegetables, and fruit trees. But unlike most founding colonists, at first they did not have to depend on their own farms for food. They had a store of food provided by the trustees. In addition, they had the gifts of livestock and rice from South Carolina, as well as some animal meat presented to them by friendly Native Americans nearby.

Although the first Georgians rarely went hungry, they did suffer badly from disease. By the summer, many were sick, and some were dying. Among those who died was the only doctor, Dr. William Cox, who was the first recorded English death in Georgia. Fortunately, a ship with new settlers, including a doctor, arrived in Savannah in July 1733. The settlers were Jews from England.

The trustees wanted Georgia to be a Protestant colony. The charter explicitly banned Catholics from settling there, but it said

Sir John Perceval, who was also called the Earl of Egmont and was president of the colony's trustees, made this list of Georgia settlers in the 1730s. Reverend John Wesley's name is listed, along with information about the colonists, including their occupations and the dates they arrived, departed, and died, if relevant.

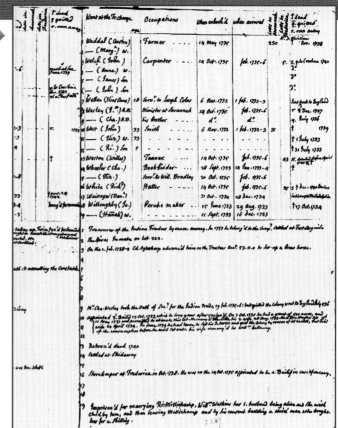

nothing about Jews. The trustees were not pleased about having Jews in Georgia, but Oglethorpe ignored their objections. The Jewish colonists stayed on in Savannah and became important settlers of the town.

The trustees were more welcoming to a group of Lutherans from Salzburg, Austria. These Protestants were escaping religious persecution in their native land, which was primarily Catholic. The Salzburgers established their own settlement, which they called Ebenezer.

A Triumphant Return

In April 1734, Oglethorpe left Georgia and headed back to England. He wanted to persuade the trustees that he needed to better

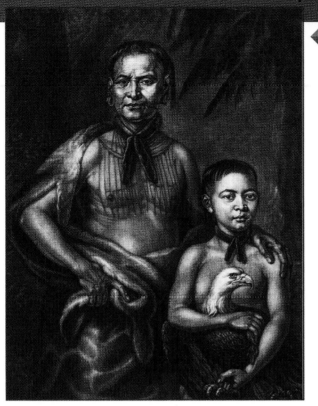

Tomochichi, leader of the Yamacraws, and his nephew, Tooanahowi, are depicted in this mezzotint around 1735–1740. The Yamacraws had been exiled from the Creek confederacy and had established a settlement on Yamacraw Bluff when Oglethorpe and the other colonists first arrived in Georgia. Oglethorpe respected Tomochichi and took him, his wife, Senawchi, and Tooanahowi and other Native Americans to England and presented them to King George II and to the trustees.

secure the colony's southern border. The news from Georgia was so encouraging to the colony's supporters in London that they greeted Oglethorpe as a hero.

But the trustees were even more excited to see the Native Americans who accompanied Oglethorpe on his trip. Traveling with him were Tomochichi, the Creek leader who had become a close friend and ally of Oglethorpe's, as well as Tomochichi's wife, his nephew, and five warriors. At the time, the English were fascinated with stories of Native Americans, so they were understandably eager to meet these visitors in person. The Creeks were honored by the trustees and even had a meeting with George II and Caroline, England's reigning king and queen.

Although Oglethorpe was eager to return to Georgia, he could not get away until late the following year. Having been granted approval for building a new southern settlement, he sailed back with some 300 settlers, including more Salzburgers. Once back in the colony, Oglethorpe set about founding his new town. Called Frederica, it was home to more than 100 settlers by the end of March 1736.

Three Laws

Oglethorpe also had to implement three new laws the trustees set down for the colony. One made it illegal to own African slaves in Georgia. To the trustees, outlawing slavery was less of a moral act than a practical ploy. South Carolina had long used slave labor to work on large plantations. This meant that plantation owners grew rich and small farmers, unable to compete, often became poor. The trustees instead wanted Georgia to be a colony made up entirely of small farmers, living on concentrated farms rather than on isolated plantations. With many farmers inhabiting a fairly small area, they could quickly form an army if Georgia was ever invaded.

The second law called for stricter trade regulations with Native Americans. The trustees believed that Georgia could be safe only if it maintained good relations with nearby groups of Native Americans. They feared that unless traders' activities were closely monitored, the traders might anger Native Americans by trying to cheat them. Almost immediately, though, South Carolinians objected to Georgia's new policy, because they did not want Georgians to horn in on their own trade with the Native Americans. Intimidated by the loud griping of South Carolinian traders, Georgia largely ignored the trustees' law governing trade with Native Americans.

The third law was one close to Oglethorpe's heart. It forbade the consumption of rum or brandy in Georgia. Again, this law

Elkaleh "Nellie" Bush Sheftall (1772–1830) was one of the Jewish women who lived in Savannah. Although she was born in Chestnut Hill, Pennsylvania, she married Moses Sheftall, whose father was one of the first children born in Savannah. The Sheftalls played significant roles in the acceptance of Jewish citizens in Savannah.

was in part designed to court the loyalty of Native American leaders, who generally did not like the English selling liquor to their people. But Oglethorpe also believed rum was bad for his colonists. He was convinced it was the source of the illness the Georgians had suffered during their first summer in America. Oglethorpe allowed the colonists to drink beer and wine, but they still wanted rum. They freely flouted the law, and the rum trade flourished.

The colonists' refusal to observe the rum ban no doubt annoyed Oglethorpe. But soon he had a worse problem to worry about. The Spanish had never given up on the idea that Georgia's lands were theirs, and they were poised to take control, even if it meant going to war.

CHAPTER 3

The War with the Spanish

Once Frederica was established, Oglethorpe toured the southern Georgia coast, accompanied by Tomochichi and a crew of about seventy Englishmen and Native Americans. In a few days, they reached an island at the mouth of the St. Johns River. There, Oglethorpe instructed his men to build a fort. He called it Fort St. George, named after the patron saint of England.

Oglethorpe was convinced that Fort St. George marked the border between Georgia and Spanish Florida. Not everyone agreed. The Spanish were furious over Oglethorpe's fort, which sat on land long claimed by Spain. More surprising, some English officials were also upset. Oglethorpe's tour had taken him far to the south of the Altamaha River, which the Georgia charter had set as the colony's southern border. Fearing the incident could spark a full-scale war with Spain, even the English prime minister, Robert Walpole, condemned Oglethorpe's action.

To London

At first, Spain was willing to look for a diplomatic solution. In October 1736, Spanish diplomats met with Oglethorpe in Frederica and negotiated a settlement. With the Treaty of Frederica, Oglethorpe promised to abandon Fort St. George. Both sides agreed to let their governments in Europe decide the exact location of the Georgia-Florida boundary.

The next month, Oglethorpe boarded a ship bound for London. The trustees, angry at his troublemaking, wanted to discuss the colony's future. Oglethorpe was also eager to meet with English officials. He was afraid the prime minister was considering handing Georgia over to Spain to avoid a conflict.

While Oglethorpe headed for England, the Georgians were growing nervous. They heard rumors that the Spanish were gathering troops and planning to invade the colony. In London, Oglethorpe used these rumors to his advantage. He wanted the English government to provide him with a regiment of soldiers for Georgia's defense. Oglethorpe warned that, without the soldiers, Georgia could fall to a Spanish army. And if Georgia were taken over by Spain, there would be nothing to stop the French from attacking the Carolinas and Virginia.

In the end, Oglethorpe was granted his regiment of 700 soldiers. He was also given the honorary title of general, but he had lost influential friends in the process. Before leaving England, he invited the trustees to an elegant dinner, but only four took the trouble to attend. King George II also had his doubts about Oglethorpe. In a meeting with the Georgian leader, the king sternly cautioned him not to do anything that would threaten England's friendship with Spain.

War Breaks Out

In September 1738, Oglethorpe and his soldiers reached Frederica, which became the regiment's base of operations. From the start, keeping control over the troops was a challenge. With little to feed the soldiers, they were on the brink of mutiny. One even shot at Oglethorpe. The bullet grazed his face, leaving a burn on Oglethorpe's cheek.

Late the next year, news reached Georgia that England and Spain were at war. The Georgia-Florida boundary dispute was, at

A VIEW of the TOWN and CASTLE of St. AUGUSTINE, and the ENGLISH CAMP before it June 20. 1740. by THO.s SILVER.

Thomas Silver engraved this map of the siege of the Castillo de San Marcos and the town of St. Augustine in 1741. The print shows Oglethorpe's soldiers' encampment (letter F), the ships blockading the city, and the cannons (letter A) firing across the Matanza River on June 20, 1740. Although Oglethorpe had originally planned to attack the Spanish colony by land and sea, when his army reached the town, there were six Spanish ships already in the harbor.

first, only a small part of the conflict. The war largely grew out of a struggle between the English and Spanish over control of trade in Spain's American colonies. The conflict was called the War of Jenkins's Ear. It took its name from an incident during which a Spanish coast guard sailor in the West Indies cut off the ear of English captain Robert Jenkins as punishment for allegedly smuggling goods off the coast of Havana.

For Oglethorpe, the war signaled a chance to make a bold move against Spanish Florida. He began building up his army, asking for help from both South Carolina and the Creek confederacy. In May 1740, Oglethorpe led about 1,000 colonists and 1,100 Native Americans south toward the Spanish stronghold at St. Augustine.

Retreat from Florida

Oglethorpe's battle plan was to attack by land and sea. But when his army reached St. Augustine, it discovered six Spanish ships in its harbor. Seeing that a sea attack would likely fail, Oglethorpe decided to surround St. Augustine, making it impossible for supplies to reach the Spanish there. His army settled in, waiting for the desperate and starving Spanish to give up.

The Spanish, though, refused to surrender. As the days passed, Oglethorpe's men grew restless as they sweated in the summer heat. Many, including Oglethorpe, became ill. Some Carolinians deserted, and many of the Creeks demanded payment from Oglethorpe while they waited to fight. With his army collapsing, Oglethorpe had little choice but to retreat. By the end of July, his men withdrew from St. Augustine and headed north to Frederica.

For the Georgians, the expedition was a failure. For Oglethorpe personally, it was also a humiliation. But worse, it had only heightened the tension between Georgia and Florida. Oglethorpe was

This drawing from the notebooks of Philip von Reck, a German who accompanied the Salzburgers to Georgia, shows the fortification of Fort St. Andrews on Cumberland Island in 1736. Oglethorpe had built the fort to help defend the British settlements in southern Georgia from the Spanish in Florida. After the British defeated the Spanish in the Battle of Bloody Marsh in 1742, the fort became less important and was later abandoned.

now convinced the Spanish would eventually invade Georgia. However, increasingly, he had trouble raising the money he needed for the colony's defense.

Attack on Frederica

In June 1742, Native American spies reported to Oglethorpe that the Spanish were heading toward Frederica. The Spanish forces originally included 7,000 men and fifty-six ships of various sizes, but because of a storm, not all the forces made it to the mainland. On July 7, the army set upon the Georgian settlement. In a series of attacks and counterattacks, the outnumbered Georgians held their ground, forcing the Spanish to fall back. Later known as the Battle of Bloody Marsh, the conflict was a much-needed victory for Oglethorpe.

Even after its retreat, the still-strong Spanish army remained a threat. Oglethorpe plotted a surprise attack, but news of his plan reached the Spanish. He then sent a messenger to carry a letter he knew would fall into Spanish hands. It said Oglethorpe was expecting fresh ships and reinforcements. The Spanish leaders did not want to take the chance of encountering an enlarged English force. Instead of staging another attack on Frederica, they turned around and headed back to St. Augustine.

The Georgians were ecstatic. Oglethorpe proclaimed July 25 as a day of thanks to God "for his great deliverance, and the end that is put to this Spanish invasion." The governors of seven colonies sent Oglethorpe letters of congratulations.

Oglethorpe's Fate

In February 1743, Oglethorpe made one last attempt to capture St. Augustine. His men shot at its fort, the Castillo de San Marcos, but they could not lure the Spanish soldiers out. Oglethorpe's army quickly returned home without inflicting much damage.

A few months later, Oglethorpe had to confront a new threat. Lieutenant Colonel William Cooke, a soldier who had served under Oglethorpe, made charges against his management of the regiment. In July, Oglethorpe sailed back to England to face a court-martial.

Eventually, Oglethorpe was cleared of all charges. He continued to attend trustee meetings from time to time. But he never returned to Frederica. His career as Georgia's leader was over.

CHAPTER 4

The outcome of the war with Spain was a great victory for Georgia. It marked the end of Spain's efforts to take military control of lands north of Florida. The Georgia colonists no longer had to worry constantly about a Spanish invasion. The war also drew the colonists closer together. Driving out the much superior Spanish force gave them a sense of shared identity. As successful defenders of their colony, they now saw themselves less as Englishmen and more as Georgians.

A Failed Vision

But the war had also taken a toll. Many colonists fled Georgia to escape the violence, causing the colony's population to drop sharply. The conflict also interfered with Georgians' ability to farm and operate businesses. With the colonists preoccupied with fighting the Spanish, Georgia struggled not just to grow but to survive.

A New Government

Amid their troubles, some Georgians began to question the trustees' authority. Unlike most English colonies, Georgia had no government body to make or even suggest laws. The only laws governing them were those set down by the trustees. In the late 1730s, more than 100 colonists, nicknamed the "malcontents," sent a document to the trustees, objecting to some of their rules. When the trustees barely responded to their protests, they moved to Charles Town. From there, the malcontents published *A True and Historical Narrative of the Colony of Georgia* (1741), a scathing criticism of the trustees' policies.

To His Excellency

James Oglethorpe, *Esq;*

General and Commander in Chief of His Majesty's Forces in SOUTH CAROLINA *and* GEORGIA; *and one of the Honourable Trustees for Establishing the Colony of* Georgia *in* AMERICA, *&c.*

May it please Your Excellency,

AS the few surviving Remains of the Colony of *Georgia* find it necessary to present the World (and in particular *Great Britain*) with a true State of that Province, from its first Rise to its present Period; Your Excellency (of all Mankind) is best entitled to the Dedication, as the principal Author of its present Strength and Affluence, Freedom and Prosperity: And tho' incontestable Truths will recommend the following *NARRA-TIVE* to the patient and attentive Reader; yet your Name, *SIR*, will be no little Ornament to the Frontispiece, and may possibly engage some courteous Perusers a little beyond it.

THAT Dedication and Flattery are synonimous, is the Complaint of every Dedicator, who concludes himself ingenuous and fortunate, if he can discover a less trite and direct Method of flattering than is usually practised; but we are happily prevented from the least Intention of this kind, by the repeated Offerings of the *Muses* and *News-Writers* to Your Excellency, in the publick Papers: 'Twere presumptuous even to dream of equalling or encreasing them; We therefore flatter ourselves, that Nothing we can advance will in the least shock Your Excellency's Modesty; not doubting but your Goodness will pardon any Deficiency of Elegance and Politeness, on account of our Sincerity, and the serious Truth we have the Honour to approach you with.

WE have seen the ancient Custom of sending forth Colonies, for the Improvement of any distant Territory, or new Acquisition, continued down to ourselves; but to Your Excellency alone it is owing, that the World is made acquainted with a Plan, highly refined from those of all former Projecters. They fondly imagin'd it necessary to communicate to such young Settle-

In 1741, a group of colonists, called the malcontents, who protested the actions of the trustees, published a pamphlet entitled *A True and Historical Narrative of the Colony of Georgia.* Patrick Tailfer, Hugh Anderson, and David Douglas, among others, wrote the document to counter claims made by William Stephens, secretary to the trustees, who had commended the trustees and their policies in an earlier report. The page pictured here, from an 1836 reprint, is the first page of the dedication that the malcontents wrote to Oglethorpe. In their humorous satire, they praised the founder of the colony for keeping them impoverished and overworked. For a partial transcription of the narrative, see pages 53–54.

The controversy caused by the malcontents' publication forced the trustees to form a new government for Georgia. In 1741, it divided the colony into two counties, one centered in Savannah and one centered in Frederica. Each county had a president and four assistants. Oglethorpe was named the president at Frederica, the first official political title he held in Georgia. William Stephens, formerly the secretary of the colony, was named the president at Savannah. After Oglethorpe's departure, the two governments were merged, and Stephens became the president of the entire colony.

White traders in the Georgia colony frequently disregarded the rules set by the trustees in dealings with the Native Americans. Native Americans traded deerskin and beaver furs for manufactured goods, such as firearms, and rum. Oglethorpe did his best to keep the settlers from drinking rum, but taverns serving it were commonly found in Savannah and Augusta.

Stephens worked hard to settle disputes among the colonists and wrote a journal to keep the trustees informed about what was happening in the colony. But Stephens had little real power and no strong desire to question the trustees. The people of Georgia, on the other hand, were increasingly willing to challenge their rulers in London.

Defying the Rules

By the 1740s, nearly all Georgians ignored the trustees' law against drinking rum. From the beginning of the colony, rum drinking was common. Oglethorpe tried his best to keep the

MARY MUSGROVE

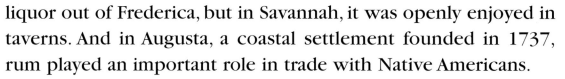

In 1749, a woman marched into Savannah escorted by 200 Creek warriors. She was Mary Musgrove, a half-Creek trader who had long been friendly with the Georgians. Musgrove was angry. She claimed that James Oglethorpe had offered her a salary for acting as his interpreter, but he had never paid her. Musgrove threatened to destroy Savannah if she did not receive her money. When the Georgia militia gathered around her, though, she backed down and left the town. Several years later, however, Musgrove took her grievances to a London courtroom. In the suit, she won title to Georgia's St. Catherines Island and a cash award of more than 2,000 English pounds.

liquor out of Frederica, but in Savannah, it was openly enjoyed in taverns. And in Augusta, a coastal settlement founded in 1737, rum played an important role in trade with Native Americans.

Almost as quickly, the Georgians abandoned the trustees' plans for what they should grow. The trustees wanted Georgia to produce olives, coffee, and other exotic foods that could be exported to England. But most of these early Georgians were artisans and tradespeople. They had enough trouble learning to grow corn, beans, squash, and other foods they needed to survive. Few had any interest in producing the exotic plants the trustees wanted them to farm.

The colonists also resented the trustees' rules about how land was distributed and owned. The trustees' surveyor was responsible for dividing the colony's land into plots with clearly defined borders. But the surveying was a slow process, and colonists often grew angry waiting for a plot. Making matters worse, the quality of the farmland varied from plot to plot. Colonists given inferior land felt they were cheated.

Other restrictions created even more hardships. No one was allowed to own more than 500 acres (202 ha). Although much of the land in Georgia was perfect for growing rice, this rule made it impossible because rice production required a large amount of land. The trustees also held that only men could own land. This meant that widows could not inherit their husband's plots, leaving them and their children unable to make a living.

In the 1740s, colonists considered these land restrictions so unfair that they refused to observe them. The trustees had little choice but to loosen the rules. Women were permitted to own land, and the maximum size of a plot rose to 2,000 acres (809 ha), allowing the rice industry to grow.

Slaves in Georgia

Many Georgians did support one of the trustees' laws: the ban on slavery in the colony. A few objected to slavery on moral grounds. But more agreed with the trustees' belief that relying on slave labor made white workers lazy. They also feared slave revolts. Many Georgians remembered the Stono Rebellion of 1739, in which some twenty-five white South Carolinians were killed by slaves.

In 1750, after mounting pressure from the rice planters, the trustees agreed to do away with the antislavery law. Growing rice required so many laborers that it was hard to make a profit unless the work was done by unpaid slaves. Even the trustees acknowledged that if Georgia was to develop a lucrative rice industry, slavery would have to be legal in the colony.

Once the ban was lifted, the slave population of Georgia grew rapidly. Within just a few years, there were more black slaves than white colonists living in the areas where rice grew best, particularly along the well-watered coastal areas.

As rice plantations grew prosperous and became vital to the colony's economy, the demand for slaves to work on the plantations increased. Georgia's trustees lifted the ban on the practice of slavery in 1750. With the introduction of slavery to Georgia, the trustees' original purpose for the colony—creating a place where small farmers could be productive—ended.

The Trustees Disband

The introduction of slavery to Georgia marked the end of the original trustees' dreams for the colony. They had imagined Georgia as a haven where England's cast-offs could be transformed into productive and responsible small farmers. In this vision of Georgia, there would be no rich people and no poor people.

But by the 1750s, Georgia looked much more like South Carolina. Like its northern neighbor, Georgia's economy was based on large plantations worked by slaves. Plantation owners enjoyed lives of leisure, while small farmers and artisans struggled just to get by.

Because of Georgia's transformation, English philanthropists lost interest in the colony. Their charitable contributions to the trustees amounted to almost nothing. The trustees had to rely exclusively on funding from the British government. But in 1751, even these funds dried up. Parliament refused to grant the trustees any money to keep Georgia going.

According to Georgia's original charter, the trustees were to run the colony until 1753. But, in 1752, the trustees faced the facts: with no money and little faith left, they decided to give up on Georgia one year early. They dissolved the trust, and Georgia became a royal colony.

CHAPTER 5

The trustees had controlled Georgia for twenty years. In that time, the colony did succeed in keeping Spanish invaders out of the English colonies. But by every other measure, Georgia had been a failure. It had grown, but very slowly, and often seemed on the verge of economic collapse.

Understandably, the Georgians were ready for a change. They were pleased when Georgia became a royal colony. They would now be ruled by a governor who was appointed by the king. They would also be allowed to form a court system and an assembly, a group of colonists charged with making laws.

A Royal Colony

The Reynolds Disaster

In October 1754, a ship carrying Captain John Reynolds, Georgia's first royal governor, sailed into Savannah's port. The entire town turned out to celebrate his arrival. With the church bells ringing, the colonists cheered and shot their guns in the air as a salute to their new ruler.

Reynolds immediately set up Georgia's assembly. It was divided into two houses. The upper house, or council, was made up of twelve men appointed by the king. The lower house was composed of elected representatives. Only men who owned at least 50 acres (20 ha) of land could vote.

After the assembly was established, Reynolds began working to improve Georgia's defenses. Since Oglethorpe's departure, there were few soldiers prepared to defend Georgia. Even worse, Frederica was in near ruins, leaving the colony's southern border largely unprotected.

Captain John Reynolds, a British naval officer, became Georgia's first royal governor in 1754. Reynolds called together Georgia's first assembly, entered into friendly agreements with the Native Americans, created courts of law, and worked to improve the colony's military defenses. He resigned in February 1757 after major disagreements with the assembly.

As Reynolds made plans to improve the military, he started running into problems with the assembly. Reynolds spent huge sums of money on his efforts. When the assemblymen questioned his policies or offered him advice, he arrogantly ignored them, alienating the colony's most important and influential leaders.

Reynolds also appointed his friend William Little to several important colonial offices. Little was widely disliked. He was accused of lying, falsifying documents, and slandering assembly members. Members of the council let officials in England know exactly how they felt about Reynolds. Because of their complaints, after serving just two and a half years, Georgia's first royal governor was recalled to England.

Turning the Colony Around

Reynolds's replacement, Henry Ellis, arrived in Georgia in 1757. Ellis was a wealthy, well-traveled man with an interest in science and natural history. Again, the people of Savannah turned out to greet their new governor. One part of the festivities, though, especially impressed Ellis. After the sun went down, the Georgians gleefully burned an effigy, or dummy, of the hated William Little. The display reminded Ellis not to make the mistakes of the previous administration. If he was to be an effective governor, he would have to treat his subjects with respect.

Ellis's style of governing quickly won over the Georgians. He got along well with the assembly. Within six months, he had the colony running more efficiently than it ever had. Ellis, however, found Georgia's weather too hot and its society too dull. After just three years, he resigned his post and returned to London.

Georgia's third royal governor was its best. Taking over as lieutenant governor in 1760 and as governor in 1761, James Wright, who was a former attorney general of South Carolina, served Georgia for the next sixteen years. Like Ellis, he was careful to earn the Georgians' trust. But unlike Ellis, he had the patience to take on the difficult and often tedious task of making Georgia into a successful colony. From the start, Wright had three goals for Georgia: to make it more secure, to increase its population, and to build the wealth of its people and government.

Securing Georgia

To improve Georgia's defenses, Wright worked to construct more forts and train its militia. But luck also played a hand in making Georgia safer. From 1754 to 1763, the English fought in the French and Indian War. The war pitted the English against the French and their Native American allies in America. No battles were fought in Georgia, but the colony benefited hugely from England's victory. By the terms of the peace treaty, England gained control of Spanish Florida and most of France's territory east of the

This engraving shows seven Cherokee men walking in St. James Garden in London in 1730. They wore British clothing that was given to them by King George II during their visit to England, in which they signed a treaty giving English traders protection in Carolina and parts of Georgia. After the French and Indian War, Governor James Wright persuaded the Creeks to cede territory to Georgia, which Wright hoped to make available to immigrants for farming.

Mississippi River. Now Georgia was no longer neighboring lands claimed by foreign nations. For the first time in its history, neither the Spanish nor the French were a threat to its borders.

The year the war ended, Wright met with Creek leaders in Augusta. There, he persuaded the Native Americans to cede about 2.4 million acres (971,246 ha) of Creek territory to Georgia. In 1773, he negotiated a second, even bigger land cession from the Creeks. Wright's careful and friendly dealings with the Creeks not only protected the Georgians from Native American attacks, they also allowed him to extend the colony's borders without warfare.

In 1763, Governor Wright wrote this proclamation, in which he announced government protection of Native American lands in the name of the king. The proclamation prohibited settlement west of the Appalachian Mountains, which would then concentrate new settlements around Augusta. For a transcription of the proclamation, see pages 54–55.

This new land was instrumental in achieving Wright's second goal of increasing the number of people in Georgia. In 1763, the colony had a population of about 10,000. In just ten years, that number had more than tripled. Some of the newcomers were immigrants from England, Ireland, and Scotland. Others were colonists from Virginia and the Carolinas, where good land was becoming scarcer. Still others were slaves, most arriving in Georgia directly from Africa.

Growing Richer

With slave labor, plantations produced rice and indigo, a plant used to make a blue dye. But most white Georgians lived on small farms, where they grew food crops and raised livestock. Some worked in the colony's lumber industry, turning Georgia's forests into wooden planks for houses and other buildings.

Under Wright's leadership, Georgians began exporting more goods than ever before. Merchants sold Georgian wood, cattle, and hogs in the West Indies in exchange for rum, sugar, and molasses. But rice was by far their most important export. In the twelve years between 1760 and 1772, the amount of rice produced by the colony rose from 4,000 to 17,000 barrels per year.

As the colony's economy grew, its people had more time for leisure and learning. Savannah remained the colony's cultural center, although Augusta, bustling with traders, offered a rowdy social life largely focused on taverns. During the period in which Georgia was a royal colony, it had more than thirty schools and at least five libraries of note. Throughout the colony, Georgians were enthusiastic readers. After 1763, in addition to books, they could read the *Georgia Gazette*, the colony's first newspaper. In the towns, Georgians could attend horse races, cricket matches, and concerts.

During the royal period, Georgia had virtually been transformed. Once a marginal colony at best, it now boasted a growing population, a vigorous economy, and a vibrant local government. Georgians also began to think of themselves differently. Not long before, they had desperately looked to England for guidance. Under Wright's administration especially, they developed more confidence in handling their own affairs. The Georgians had come to regard themselves—not the faraway English—as the people who knew best how to mold the colony's future.

CHAPTER 6

Growing Independent

In the 1760s, Georgia was doing better than ever. Both its population and land base were growing. Farming and other industries were thriving. And in Governor James Wright, it finally had a strong leader completely devoted to the colony and its people. In September 1765, John Bartram, a naturalist who was visiting Georgia, noted that Wright was "universally respected by all the inhabitants. They can hardly say enough in his praise." Although most Georgians were still singing the royal governor's praises, some began challenging English authority for the first time.

The Stamp Act

After the French and Indian War, England reexamined some of its policies concerning America. The war had been expensive. Because it was fought to protect the colonies, England decided the colonists should pay for it. The British parliament began passing a series of acts to levy new taxes on its colonial subjects.

Colonists throughout America resisted these taxes. They were especially enraged by the Stamp Act of 1765. This act placed a tax on all printed material, including newspapers and legal documents. A special stamp was affixed to paper to show the tax was paid. At first, Georgians seemed to accept the Stamp Act. Although the *Georgia Gazette* reported on other colonies' opposition, Georgia neglected to send a representative to New York, where the colonies held a Stamp Act congress to discuss the issue.

This is the front page of the *Georgia Gazette* from January 17, 1770. The *Georgia Gazette* began publication in 1763 in Savannah and was the first newspaper printed in Georgia. It suspended publication on February 7, 1776, because of the American Revolution, and resumed publication on January 30, 1783, as the *Gazette of the State of Georgia*.

But the day before the Stamp Act was to go into effect, a mob gathered in Savannah. The crowd burned an effigy of a stamp master, the official charged with enforcing the law. The protest presented Governor Wright with a problem. Implementing the Stamp Act was sure to inspire more mob action. But if he bowed to the colonists' will, he would be violating his pledge to uphold English law in Georgia.

Selling Stamps

For a time, Wright had an excuse for not implementing the Stamp Act. There was no stamp master in Georgia. A few Georgians joined the rebel group called the Sons of Liberty to keep it that way. They learned a stamp master was due to arrive in Savannah on January 3, 1766. The day before, the Sons of Liberty marched toward Wright's house. He met them outside with a musket in his hand, and the group backed down.

With Wright's blessing, some sixty ships with stamped paper entered Savannah's port. These stamps were the only ones sold in all of the thirteen colonies before the Stamp Act was repealed in 1766. Because of his broad support among Georgians, Wright had been the only colonial governor able to enforce the law at all.

The crisis was over, but it had left Wright shaken. It was clear that the Georgians were no longer docilely loyal to England. Wright suspected that this would not be the last time they would challenge his authority.

Trouble with the Assembly

Georgia was fairly calm for the next year. But in 1767, England again angered the colonists by passing the Townshend Acts. These laws placed taxes on goods imported from England.

Massachusetts wanted the other colonies to support an official objection to the tax. Wright was afraid the lower house of the assembly might do it. Before it could even consider the matter, he dismissed the assembly. The councilors of the upper house were still fully behind Wright. But as the governor's action suggests, he was losing the loyalty of the lower house leaders.

Wright's biggest confrontation with the assembly came in 1771. The lower house elected Noble Jones to be its speaker. Jones was a leader of the antitax faction. Fearing Jones would make trouble, Wright refused to allow him to be the speaker

Sir James Wright (1716–1785), Georgia's third royal governor, first came to America in 1730 when his father became chief justice of the colony of South Carolina. Wright became a lawyer and practiced law in South Carolina before he was appointed royal governor in 1760. Most of the colonists respected Wright as a leader. He supported the settlement of Georgia's frontier. Over the years he bought eleven plantations, which totaled more than 25,000 acres (10,117 ha).

and dissolved the assembly. The governor set off for England, where he stayed for a year and a half. While he was away, his friend James Habersham ruled the colony. The lower house twice voted for Jones as speaker, and Habersham twice vetoed its decision.

Tensions Rise

When Wright returned to Georgia in 1773, he still had enough supporters to receive a warm welcome. But an English tax on tea soon provided a new test to Wright's popularity. In several colonies, most notably in Massachusetts, protesters staged "tea parties," during which they destroyed taxable tea imported from England.

Noble W. Jones, who was born in England, came to Savannah in 1733. He studied medicine and owned a rice plantation along the Ogeechee River. In 1755, Jones was elected to the lower house of the assembly, called the Commons House. As a vocal opponent of the British taxation actions, particularly the Stamp Act and the Intolerable Acts, Noble became Governor Wright's major adversary. He was elected to the Second Continental Congress as one of Georgia's delegates.

News of these protests fired up Georgia's most rebellious leaders. They called a meeting in Savannah in August 1774 and drafted a statement objecting to England's abuses. Wright countered by asking influential friends in the colony to write their own statements in praise of English rule.

In January 1775, the rebel faction went a step further. It established the Provincial Congress as an alternative to the officially